Maat

Egyptian Goddess of Justice and Harmony

Table of Contents

Introduction

D o you want to learn more about the Egyptian goddess Maat and her enduring legacy? Have you ever wondered what principles she stood for and how her impact can still be felt today?

An ancient Egyptian deity, Maat was the symbol of order and cosmic harmony that kept the universe running smoothly. In the culture of Ancient Egypt, she was viewed as a significant part of the world-making creation process and lauded for her strength in upholding social balance and justice. Her legacy lives on to this day, setting an example of fairness and righteousness that all civilizations should strive towards. Maat is an incredible female figure whose wisdom continues to teach us crucial values even thousands of years after her existence in Ancient Egypt.

Maat held an impressive role in ancient Egypt, as evidenced by her presence in artwork from tombs to temples. She was considered so imperative for keeping the country at peace that even her image would bring a sense of harmony. People viewed balance and justice as essential values, prerequisites to living in a safe and tranquil nation, and looked to Maat to make sure they were upheld. Even when the lands were filled with evidence of unrest, the importance of Maat was never forgotten.

Interestingly, her symbol was a feather that indicated truth. Pharaohs had their hearts weighed against this symbol to signify that their rule embodied these values. Over time, her awe-inspiring presence has persisted, guided by her infinite spirit, which existed outside of time and space. This enigmatic concept of timelessness made her even more powerful and truly immortal to believers, inspiring all sorts of stories about her unsurpassable power in classical mythology. Consequently, Maat remains worshipped today amongst ancient civilization and wider spiritual communities due to her mysterious ability to transcend both temporal and physical boundaries. Her beauty and grace will remain untouched by our physical world for millennia to come.

In this guide, we will explore Maat's origins, the gods and goddesses associated with her, the principles of Maat that defined Egyptian society, festivals celebrating her, and ways to honor her legacy. We will also discuss ways to offer prayers and sacrifices to her still today. By the end of this guide, you'll be familiar with Maat's influence and understand how her principles are still valued today. You'll be able to practice honoring Maat in your own life to ensure balance and justice in the world. So, let's dive into discovering more about this amazing goddess!

Chapter 1:

The Origins of Maat

Maat is an ancient Egyptian concept, often symbolized by a goddess, which dates back to the dawn of civilization. In its most basic form, it means "truth" and "justice," although the Egyptian understanding was much deeper. To the Egyptians, it involved a moral code and personal responsibility, various acts of goodwill and fairness, and general order such as balance and harmony. This worldview provided the backdrop for everything from their daily lives to their majestic hieroglyphs carved on temple walls. It is a lasting legacy that still resonates today as we strive to create a safer, more equitable world.

This chapter will discuss the ancient Egyptian mythology surrounding Maat, from her creation to her role in the afterlife. It will cover her origins, her role in ancient Egyptian religion and mythology, and the cult of Maat that developed as a result. The chapter will also explore Maat's impact on societies, such as its influence on the law and justice systems. With this knowledge, we can gain greater insight into how the Egyptians viewed truth, justice, and morality.

Maat's Creation

Egypt is a country that is rich in history, but its mythology is equally fascinating. Maat, the goddess of truth, justice, and harmony, is one of the most revered symbols in ancient Egyptian mythology. Her name translates to "that which is straight," and she was one of the most influential deities in the pantheon. Maat's creation was so vital that it was believed to have set the standard for how the world should function. Let's explore the magic of Maat's creation and gain a better understanding of the role she played in ancient Egypt.

The Myth of Maat's Creation

According to Egyptian mythology, Maat's creation story starts with the god of creation, Atum. He created himself from the primordial waters of chaos and gave birth to two children, Shu, and Tefnut. Shu represented the air, while Tefnut was the goddess of moisture. They, in turn, gave birth to a son named Geb and a daughter named Nut. Geb was the god of the earth, and Nut was the goddess of the sky. Geb and Nut then gave birth to four children, including Maat. She was considered the embodiment of truth and balance and essential in ensuring the universe remained in harmony.

The Symbolism of Maat

Maat was often depicted wearing a feather on her head, symbolizing the balance of the universe. Her feather was used in the judgment of the dead, where it was placed on a scale against the heart of the deceased. If the heart was heavier than the feather, the person would be deemed to have lived a life of imbalance and would be sentenced to an eternity of suffering. In contrast, if the heart was lighter than the feather, the person would be considered to have lived a life in balance and would be granted eternal life.

Maat Today

Today, Maat is still a symbol of balance and order. Her teachings continue to inspire those who seek to live a life of integrity and morality. The Egyptian goddess of truth remains a beloved figure in modern culture, with her image appearing in artwork, jewelry, and other media. Her role as the goddess of truth, justice, and harmony is an inspiration to those seeking to lead a life of balance and order. Whether it's through the symbolism of her feather or the concept of living a just and ethical life, Maat continues to be a part of our cultural legacy.

The Role of Maat in Ancient Egyptian Religion and Mythology

To most people, "Maat" may sound like an odd-sounding word from an ancient language. However, Maat was much more than just a word for the Egyptian people. It was an all-encompassing concept that governed their religious beliefs, everyday lives, and society as a whole. Let's dive deep into the role of Maat in ancient Egyptian religion and mythology. We'll explore what Maat is, how it was personified, and its significance in Egyptian culture. So, sit back, relax, and let us take you on a journey through ancient Egyptian history.

Maat was a central concept in ancient Egyptian religion, believed to be the foundation of the universe. The term Maat can be interpreted as "truth," "order," "justice," and "balance." It was believed that Maat was incorporated into every aspect of daily life, from individual conduct and ethics to governing the country. Maat was vital to the Egyptians' belief that they lived in a harmonious universe governed by laws rather than chance.

In ancient Egyptian mythology, Maat was personified as a goddess who was the daughter of the god of creation, Ra. She was depicted as a tall and slender woman wearing a winged headdress or as an ostrich feather, symbolizing truth. One of her most vital roles was to weigh the deceased's heart against her feather in the afterlife judgment to determine whether or not the individual was worthy of entering the afterlife.

Maat was a crucial element in the Egyptian concept of justice. She played a role in determining the rightness or wrongness of an action, and her followers believed that by living a life of balance and harmony, they would be rewarded in the afterlife. Maat was also the goddess of morality and ethics and was responsible for maintaining the order of the universe. Her presence ensured that Egypt remained stable and prosperous.

Maat also played a crucial role in maintaining social and political order in ancient Egypt. The pharaohs of Egypt were believed to be the living embodiment of Maat, and therefore it was their duty to ensure that order was maintained throughout the country. Any decision they made had to be in line with the principles of Maat, which meant that they had to act justly, compassionately, and in the best interest of their subjects.

Another significant role of Maat was in the Nile flood cycle. It was believed that the rich flood plains of Egypt were a gift from Maat, and the Nile was personified by her tears. The annual Nile flood cycle added to the fertility of the soil, which in turn supported agriculture and the livelihoods of the people. Maat was also believed to govern the laws of nature, like the rising and setting of the sun and moon and the changing of the seasons.

The Cult of Maat

The ancient Egyptian civilization is famous for its incredible art, religious practices, and mystifying belief systems. One such belief system is the Cult of Maat, a highly sophisticated and complex set of beliefs that governed Egyptian life for over 3,000 years. In this section, we will introduce you to the fascinating beliefs of the cult of Maat and explore its impact on ancient Egyptian society.

The Cult of Maat was a religious philosophy that revolved around the idea of balance and order. The ancient Egyptians believed that the universe was in a constant state of flux and that this change could be neutralized by maintaining balance and harmony in all areas of life. The cult of Maat had many different teachings, rituals, and practices, but they all revolved around the central themes of balance and order.

One of the most significant rituals of the cult was the "Weighing of the Heart" ceremony. This ceremony took place after death, during judgment in the afterlife. The deceased's heart was weighed against Maat's feather, representing the principle of balance. If the heart were heavy with sin, it would outweigh the feather, and the soul would be condemned. However, if the heart were pure and light, the soul would pass through to the afterlife.

The cult of Maat was not simply a religious system; it was a way of life. The ancient Egyptians believed that balance and order should be maintained in all aspects of life, from the political system to the daily routines of individuals. The Cult's teachings influenced the building of the pyramids, the design of temples, and even how people dressed and ate. The ancient Egyptians believed maintaining balance and harmony was essential for living a good life and achieving salvation in the afterlife.

The impact of the cult of Maat can still be felt today. Many of its teachings, including the importance of balance and justice, have influenced modern legal systems. The concept of weighing a person's actions against a set of rules is still used in modern courts. The psychological impact of the cult's teachings can also be seen in modern society. Many stress the importance of maintaining balance and harmony in one's life to achieve security and peace of mind.

The cult of Maat is a testament to the incredible sophistication and complexity of ancient Egyptian civilization. Its teachings and practices reflect a society that tried to maintain balance and harmony in all aspects of life. Even today, the impact of the Cult can still be felt in modern legal systems and the psychology of modern society. The cult of Maat is a fascinating subject that deserves further exploration and study.

In conclusion, the role of Maat in ancient Egyptian religion and mythology was all-encompassing. It was an abstract yet vital concept that governed everything in Egyptian society, from individual behavior to political and natural laws. The goddess Maat was the personified form of this concept, and her role in the afterlife judgment, social order, and natural phenomena was of great significance. Understanding the concept of Maat is essential in comprehending ancient Egyptian culture and beliefs. Maat was the pillar on which their entire way of life rested, and it played a crucial role in shaping their civilization.

Chapter 2:

Maat's Impact on Egyptian Society

Maat was an integral part of ancient Egyptian society, influencing many aspects of every-day life. Through this concept of truth, order, and morality in the universe, the Egyptians sought to lead a balanced life that would bring them peace and prosperity. This could be seen in their architecture, with a focus on symmetry in its design and construction. In terms of religion, priests observed certain rituals to keep Maat in balance and ward off potential chaos between gods and men. Its impact on literature was immortalized in classic works featuring stories of gods or historical events, which espoused these values through moral lessons for readers.

Ultimately, Maat guided Egyptians to lead fulfilling and meaningful lives. This chapter will discuss the influence of Maat on everyday life and how it shaped their legal system. It will also explore its impact on art and literature, as these were significant forms of expression that allowed the culture to uphold these values. This chapter will discuss how Maat's principles of justice and harmony influenced the daily lives of Egyptians. Through this, readers will better understand how ancient Egyptian society was shaped by these concepts at all levels. By the end of this chapter, you will better appreciate how Maat helped define how the ancient Egyptians lived and interacted with the world around them.

Maat in Everyday Life

The concept of Maat was embodied by the goddess of the same name, who was responsible for maintaining order and ensuring that everything ran smoothly. But Maat is not just a long-lost concept from Egyptian mythology. It's a set of principles that can be applied to our daily lives. In this section, we'll explore how you can incorporate the principles of Maat into your everyday life to promote balance, harmony, and justice.

1. Recognize the Interconnectedness of All Things

One of the most influential principles of Maat is the idea that everything in the universe is interconnected. This means that the well-being of one thing is intimately tied to the well-being of everything else. We can think more holistically about our lives and actions when we recognize this interconnectedness. We can make choices that promote the health and well-being of all things rather than just our own needs. We can also foster greater empathy and compassion for others, recognizing that their well-being is as significant as ours.

2. Embrace Balance and Harmony

Another key principle of Maat is the importance of balance and harmony. This means striving for a state where everything is in equilibrium and working together harmoniously. In our personal lives, this might mean finding a balance between work and leisure or between our physical, emotional, and spiritual needs. It might also mean working to resolve conflicts in our relationships so that everyone can communicate openly and honestly. When we embrace balance and harmony, we create a more peaceful and fulfilling life for ourselves and those around us.

3. Seek Justice

The concept of justice is also central to Maat. In ancient Egypt, this meant ensuring everyone was treated fairly, and those in power were held accountable for their actions. In our everyday lives, justice might mean standing up for someone being treated unfairly, advocating for policies that promote equality and justice, or simply treating others with respect and kindness. When we seek justice, we create a more just and equitable world for all.

4. Practice Self-Reflection

Self-reflection is an integral part of Maat, as it allows us to take stock of our actions and align them with the principles of balance, harmony, and justice. By examining our behaviors, we can identify areas where we may be out of balance or causing harm to others. We can then work to correct these imbalances and become more aligned with the principles of Maat. This might involve practicing mindfulness, journaling, or seeking feedback from others. When we practice self-reflection, we become more aware of ourselves and our impact on the world.

5. Cultivate Gratitude

Finally, cultivating gratitude is an essential part of living Maat. When we are grateful for what we have, we are less likely to take it for granted or seek more than we need. Gratitude also helps us stay grounded in the present moment rather than constantly striving for something more. We can cultivate gratitude by practicing mindfulness, keeping a gratitude journal, or simply taking a few moments each day to appreciate the good things in our lives. When we cultivate gratitude, we live in greater harmony with the world.

Incorporating the principles of Maat into our everyday lives can help us live more balanced, harmonious, and just lives. By recognizing the interconnectedness of all things, embracing balance and harmony, seeking justice, practicing self-reflection, and cultivating gratitude, we can create a more fulfilling and meaningful life for ourselves and those around us. So, let us strive to embody the principles of Maat in our daily lives and contribute to a more balanced, harmonious, and just world.

Maat and the Law

The concept of Maat was not just a divine principle, but it influenced every aspect of Egyptian life, including their legal system. Maat was believed to be the foundation of Egyptian law, reflecting the balance between order and chaos. The law was not just a set of rules but a way to maintain the harmony of the universe.

According to Maat, every action has a consequence, and the law was designed to ensure that these consequences were just and fair. The Egyptian legal system was based on principles of equity, fairness, and impartiality. The judge's duty was to make sure that the law was applied without bias or favoritism. Punishments were not just intended to punish but to deter others from committing the same offense.

Maat was not just a legal principle but also a way of life for the ancient Egyptians. It was a fundamental belief that guided their daily lives. Maat was the underlying principle of their moral code, and it was believed that those who lived by Maat would have a successful afterlife. This belief was so strong that it influenced how the Egyptians buried their dead.

The Book of the Dead, a collection of magical spells believed to guide the soul through the afterlife, emphasized the importance of living by Maat.

The concept of Maat remains relevant today, and it has influenced the legal systems of many countries. The principles of equity, impartiality, and fairness are still the foundation of modern legal systems. The concept of Maat can also be applied in our daily lives. It reminds us to act with integrity, honesty, and sincerity and to strive for balance and harmony in all aspects of our lives.

The Influence of Maat on Art and Literature

The ancient Egyptians were known for their great minds and incredible culture, and one of the most influential concepts to come out of their civilization was Maat. This guiding force, which embodied justice, truth, and balance, significantly impacted not just their religious beliefs but also art and literature. In this section, we'll delve into the ways Maat spurred creativity and explore how its influence continues to be seen in the work of artists and writers today.

To understand how Maat influenced the world of arts and literature, we must first examine its role in ancient Egyptian life. Ancient Egyptians believed that while Maat was inherently within the universe, it could also be upheld or violated by humans through their deeds and actions. This idea of Maat as a guiding principle lent itself to various forms of expression, from stunning sculptures that depicted the goddess herself to literary works like hymns and poetry that praised her strengths.

One genre of literature that Maat greatly influenced was wisdom literature, which the ancient Egyptians believed held profound truths about the world and human behavior. Texts like the 'Instructions of Merikare' and the 'Instructions of Amenemhat' were both written as guides for young rulers to follow, stressing the importance of upholding justice and fairness in their reign. These ancient books were filled with Maat-based ideals, teaching the reader about the balance between human and divine powers and the importance of maintaining order and stability.

Maat's influence can also be seen in the fine arts, particularly in the form of tomb paintings, carvings, and reliefs. These works of art often de-picted the deceased in a state of judgment before Osiris, the god of the dead. But at the same time, Maat was always present, with a feather, which was the goddess's symbol, held up against the heart of the deceased as a measure of their righteousness. This symbolism is a powerful example of how Maat's principles were embedded in everyday life, even in death.

Another interesting thing about the influence of Maat on art and literature is how it has spread across cultures and periods. One of the most famous exam-ples is the concept of truth and justice in Shakespeare's "Hamlet," which could easily be seen as a modern take on Maat. Also, in the work of writer and philosopher Jean Baudrillard, who wrote about "the transparency of evil," there's a clear correlation between his concepts and Maat's balancing principles. Even contemporary art forms like music have drawn on the meaning of Maat, with hip-hop artists like Jay-Z and Kendrick Lamar incorporating the goddess's principles into their lyrics and live performances.

In conclusion, the influence of Maat on art and literature has been incredibly diverse and long-lasting. From the ancient tombs of the Egyptian pharaohs to modern music, Maat has played a significant role in inspiring people to create art that reflects the goddess's ideals of justice, balance, and truth. It's clear that even after thousands of years, Maat continues to inspire creatives across the globe, cementing her status as a timeless force of nature that will always have a place in our hearts and minds.

The ancient Egyptians believed that Maat was the foundation of their legal system, reflecting their belief in balance, harmony, and truth. Maat was not just a divine principle but a way of life that guided their daily lives. The principles of equity, impartiality, and fairness that were the foundation of Egyptian law remain relevant today, and they have influenced the legal systems of many countries. The concept of Maat teaches us to act with integrity, honesty, and sincerity and to strive for balance and harmony in all aspects of our lives!

Chapter 3:

Gods and Goddesses Associated with Maat

Ancient Egyptian gods and goddesses were intricately linked to the concept of Maat. Many gods, like Isis and Hathor, were strongly associated with preserving Maat, who represented unity and justice within the cosmic and social order. Another powerful protector deity, Sekhmet demonstrated her watchful guardianship by spewing fiery warnings against those who threatened Maat. Even Sobek, the god of crocodiles, asserted his divine presence unexpectedly by defending the land against harm or invasion.

Ancient Egyptians believed that the gods watched over them as custodians of righteousness so that life on earth could be lived with harmony and balance. This chapter will take a closer look at the individual roles of these gods and goddesses in Egyptian mythology, and we will begin by looking at Thoth, the god of wisdom and writing. Then, we will explore Anubis as the god of the afterlife, followed by Isis and her role as goddess of magic and healing. We will also examine Hathor's association with joy and fertility and, finally, Sekhmet's relationship with war and vengeance. Together, these gods and goddesses represent unique Maat aspects essential to preserving ancient civilization.

Thoth - God of Wisdom and Writing

When it comes to the remarkable gods and goddesses of ancient Egypt, Thoth is undoubtedly among the most fascinating. According to Egyptian mythology, he is the god of wisdom, writing, and record-keeping, among other things, and he is often portrayed with the head of an ibis bird or a baboon. Let's take a look at who Thoth was, what he represented, and his association with Maat, the goddess of justice and truth.

Overview

Thoth was a very significant god in ancient Egypt, and he played a crucial role in worshipping the people. He was the patron god of scribes and was responsible for the development of hieroglyphic writing, the written language in ancient Egypt. In addition to this, Thoth was also known as the god who invented mathematics, astronomy, and magic.

Roles

Thoth was also the scribe of the gods and was responsible for recording the judgment of the dead in the Book of the Dead. He was portrayed as a god with a papyrus scroll and a palette, the necessary tools for Egyptian scribes of his time. Thoth's role as a scribe to the gods represents the importance of recording and preserving ancient knowledge and wisdom.

Thoth's association with writing made him a revered god among the ancient Egyptians, and his powers were called upon when they were faced with problems that could not be solved by ordinary means. Writers, scholars, and other intellectuals would invoke Thoth's name to seek inspiration, guidance, and knowledge. He was considered to be the ultimate embodiment of intellectual capability and learning.

Association with Maat

The association between Thoth and Maat is an essential one. Maat was the keeper of balance and order in ancient Egypt, and Thoth was the one who recorded the deeds of the people to ensure they remained just and true. The ancient Egyptians believed that Thoth and Maat worked together to bring about a peaceful and prosperous society. It was considered that they were the ultimate guardians of truth and justice.

Thoth's role in ancient Egypt was significant, and his association with writing, wisdom, and justice made him a powerful and influential god. The ancient Egyptians believed that Thoth's knowledge and intellect were beyond mortal comprehension, and they revered him as the keeper of ancient wisdom, truth, and knowledge. Thoth's influence remains evident in modern times, and his legacy as the god of wisdom and writing will continue to inspire future generations.

Anubis - God of the Afterlife

Ancient Egyptian mythology is full of curious tales about their pantheon of gods, goddesses, and religious practices. Among these fascinating figures is Anubis, the god of the afterlife and embalming. Often depicted with the head of a jackal and the body of a human, Anubis served a critical role in ensuring that souls could pass safely from the living world to the afterlife. In this section, we'll look closer at Anubis, the god of the afterlife, in association with Maat.

Overview

Anubis was one of the most influential gods in Ancient Egyptian mythology because he was closely associated with the process of death and the afterlife. Typically, Anubis was depicted in Ancient Egyptian art as a jackal-headed figure with a sleek, muscular body. Some experts argue that Anubis was represented as a jackal because they were scavengers that fed on dead bodies. As such, they were associated with death but also represented protection and guarding tombs.

Roles

Anubis was tasked with performing several sacrosanct duties, including weighing the hearts of the deceased against the feather of Maat. Anubis was also closely associated with embalming, a process that prevented the body from decaying and ensured its preservation for the afterlife. Priests and other specialized people would use a variety of techniques to cleanse and purify the body, removing vital organs and wrapping them with linen. Anubis was often present during this process, and experts in the field believe that priests might have called upon him to protect their work and ensure the soul's safe transition into the afterlife.

Association with Maat

Anubis's reputation as an all-important god of the afterlife was cemented by his association with the goddess Maat. Not only did Maat's feather play a central part in the weighing of the heart ceremony, but her divine principles and supreme truths were also critical to the proper preparation for burial. Individuals had to ensure that their lives abided by Maat's principles, which included obeying the law, being honest, and not indulging in evil actions. In doing so, they would ensure that their hearts would weigh no heavier than the feather of Maat in the afterlife.

Anubis, the god of the afterlife, played a central role in Ancient Egyptian culture and mythology. His influence continued to grow over time, and he eventually became one of the most influential figures in the religion. Despite his jackal-headed appearance, Anubis was revered and respected as an all-powerful protector of the dead who oversaw the Weighing of the Heart ceremony and embalming. His association with Maat was also vital, and the two figures helped facilitate passage into the afterlife. Overall, the myths surrounding Anubis are still fascinating and continue to intrigue scholars and enthusiasts alike.

Isis - Goddess of Magic and Healing

Since ancient times, Isis has been known as a powerful goddess of magic and healing. This magnificent goddess was one of the most popular goddesses in ancient Egypt, and her followers believe that she still exhibits a strong presence to this day. Isis is often depicted as a kind, nurturing, and strong figure with remarkable powers that can provide love, protection, and healing to those in need. In this section, we'll dive deeper into Isis, her role in

Egyptian mythology, her association with Maat, and the meaning behind her symbolism.

Overview

Isis was considered one of the most renowned goddesses in Egyptian mythology. She was known to be the wife of Osiris and mother to Horus, who later became the king of Egypt. Isis was recognized for her magical powers. Her legend includes a significant role in the story of Osiris, wherein she was the one who brought him back to life using her magic. Isis was also a goddess of healing, and her followers believed she could give them the strength to recover from any ailment.

Roles

The symbol of Isis is often represented as a winged goddess wearing a solar disc and cow horns on her head. She is also depicted with a headdress decorated with a cobra, representing her powers of healing and protection. Isis is often shown holding a lotus, a symbol of rebirth, representing her ability to give life back to the dead. Overall, Isis's symbols epitomize her power to bring life to those in need.

Association with Maat

Isis was closely associated with Maat, the goddess of balance and harmony. Maat represented divine order, and her association with Isis was a testament to her deep connection with justice and harmony. This association further proves the character of Isis, known for her wisdom and ability to shape the world around her. This relationship between Isis and Maat symbolizes the importance of balance, order, and ethics in Egyptian culture.

Her connection with Maat signifies the importance of balance and ethics in Egyptian culture, while her symbolism represents her power to give life and provide healing to those in need. It's no wonder that Isis still exists in many people's lives, even in modern times. Her representation inspires us to strive for balance and use our wisdom to shape and heal the world.

Hathor - Goddess of Joy and Fertility

Ancient Egyptians worshipped many gods and goddesses; among them was Hathor, the goddess of joy and fertility. Hathor is a significant deity that symbolizes nurturing, love, dancing, and music.

Her association with Maat, the goddess of truth and justice, is particularly striking, and together they represent a balance between pleasure and order. Let's uncover more about the myths, symbols, and importance of Hathor and her connection to Maat.

Mythology of Hathor

Hathor has a rich mythology that involves multiple characters and stories. One of the most notable legends is how she nearly destroyed the world from anger but was pacified by drinking beer with red ochre that turned it into a reddish color. Another story involves how she helped Ra, the sun god, defeat his enemies by transforming into a lioness and slaughtering them. Additionally, Hathor played a significant role in the afterlife, helping the dead transition to the underworld by guiding them through the perilous journey. She was also known as the mother of the pharaohs, and it was said that she breastfed them and nurtured them as her children.

Symbols of Hathor

Hathor had several symbols that represented her power and authority. The most common symbol is the cow, representing her nurturing and maternal nature. She also had a crown with cow horns and a solar disk in the center, symbolizing her link to the heavens and the sun god Ra. Other symbols of Hathor include a sistrum, a musical instrument that represents joy and merriment, and a menat necklace, which denotes fertility and childbirth.

Association with Maat

Maat and Hathor shared a close relationship in Ancient Egyptian mythology. Maat was the goddess of truth, order, and justice, while Hathor represented joy and love. Together, they symbolized the perfect balance between pleasure and order, and their connection was seen as vital in maintaining social harmony. In many Egyptian texts and artifacts, such as temple walls and tomb paintings, Hathor and Maat were often depicted together, with Hathor's joyful and auspicious nature contrasting Maat's somber demeanor.

In conclusion, Hathor, the goddess of joy and fertility, affirms the importance of balancing pleasure and order, and her association with Maat illustrates the significance of maintaining social harmony. Her mythology and symbols are a testament to the Ancient Egyptians' rich cultural heritage and their beliefs about the divine. Hathor's significance transcends time, and her influence can still be felt in modern-day society, particularly in the arts and music industry, where her symbolisms inspire creativity, positivity, and love.

Sekhmet - Goddess of War and Vengeance

Egyptian mythology is replete with gods and goddesses, each symbolizing a particular aspect of life. One such goddess is Sekhmet, a powerful warrior goddess and a symbol of war and vengeance. However, Sekhmet is also closely associated with Maat, the goddess of order, balance, and justice. In this section, we will explore the stories and symbols of Sekhmet and how her power can be invoked to bring balance and harmony to our lives.

Overview

Sekhmet is a fierce lioness-headed goddess often depicted wielding a bow and arrow or holding the symbol of life, the ankh. She is known for her ability to unleash chaos, destruction, and vengeance upon her enemies. However, Sekhmet's role is not simply one of destruction. She is also a powerful healer who can be called up to help us overcome illness and disease. Her fiery nature is both destructive and life-giving, a powerful reminder of the duality of all things.

Mythology of Sekhmet

In Egyptian mythology, Sekhmet is sometimes called the "Eye of Ra," a title that reflects her connection to the sun god. It is said that Sekhmet was unleashed upon the enemies of Ra, but in her fury, she threatened to destroy all of creation. To calm her down, the other gods poured beer mixed with red dye into the Nile, which she mistook for blood, and drank until she was pacified. This story shows the power of Sekhmet, and the lengths the gods were willing to go to appease her.

Invoking Sekhmet

To invoke the power of Sekhmet, you can create an altar dedicated to her, which can include a statue or image of her and offerings such as fresh flowers, candles, or incense. You can also meditate on her name, which means "the powerful one." This can help you tap into her fiery energy and bring it into your life, helping you to overcome obstacles, heal from illness, or bring about much-needed change.

Association with Maat

The association with Maat is also crucial, as Sekhmet represents the fire and fury necessary to bring about change and restore balance. It is said that when Sekhmet is out of control, Maat is called upon to restore balance and harmony. Together, these two goddesses symbolize the importance of balance in all aspects of life, reminding us that sometimes chaos and destruction are necessary to bring about change.

Sekhmet is a powerful goddess, a symbol of war and vengeance, but also of healing and balance. The stories and symbols associated with her remind us of the importance of balance in all aspects of life and how sometimes chaos and destruction must occur to bring about change. To invoke the power of Sekhmet, you can create an altar, meditate on her name, or simply honor her in your daily life. Tapping into her fiery energy can unleash your power and bring balance and harmony into your life.

This chapter explored the various gods and goddesses associated with Maat, including Hathor and Sekhmet. Ancient Egypt saw these gods as symbols of order, balance, and justice that still resonate in our modern world. Symbols like the ankh remind us of the importance of harmony and balance in all aspects of life. The stories of these gods and goddesses, including Sekhmet's role as the Eye of Ra, also show us how chaos and destruction can sometimes be necessary to bring about change and restore order.

By invoking their power through an altar or meditation, we can tap into the fiery energy of these goddesses and use it to our advantage in our own lives. Learning about the gods and goddesses associated with Maat provides a better understanding of how to bring balance and harmony into our lives. Through their stories and symbols, these gods remind us of the power of chaos and destruction and the importance of order and justice. By invoking their energy through an altar or meditation, we can use their power to bring balance and harmony into our lives.

Chapter 4:

Principles of Maat

The ancient Egyptian goddess Maat was revered as the originator of cosmic order, and her principles still hold a significant value in our modern world. The core tenets of Maat's philosophy revolve around integrity, respect for others, honesty in one's words and deeds, upholding justice while punishing wrongdoing, and ensuring that each person strives to do the right thing in any situation. By consciously striving to uphold these guiding ideals in our lives, we can invoke a greater sense of balance within ourselves and create more harmony with each other.

Living our lives with respect for Maat's moral code allows us to nurture kindness, trustworthiness, fairness, dignity, and compassion. These ideals move our society forward in a positive direction and create a more peaceful, collaborative world. This chapter will explore the seven principles of Maat, the spiritual implications of Maat's philosophy, ethical considerations from her teachings, and how to incorporate them into our daily lives.

The 7 Principles of Maat

Have you ever felt like life is a bit out of balance? Maybe you're struggling to find meaning, happiness, or purpose. Perhaps you've experienced some inner turmoil and chaos. Well, ancient Egyptians had a secret to keep their lives in harmony. The principles of Maat helped them find balance and create a just and equitable society. Maat's seven principles are still relevant today, and anyone can apply them to their lives. Here's everything you need to know about these foundational principles.

1. Truth (Justice or Righteousness)

Truth is the foundation of Maat. It means being true to yourself and living with integrity, honesty, and transparency. It also means seeking and upholding justice, fairness, and balance in all aspects of life. In practice, truth means keeping your promises, being honest in your interactions, and not deceiving others for personal gain. It also means being willing to stand up for what is right and just, even in the face of adversity.

2. Balance

Balance is the fundamental principle of Maat, representing the concept of harmony and equilibrium in our lives. Balance means we strive for the middle ground, avoiding excesses and embracing moderation. When we live in balance, we focus on the present moment, knowing that we can't control everything but can control our responses. We need to be aware of our thoughts and emotions so that we can navigate through the ups and downs of life.

3. Order

Order is the manifestation of Maat's principles, represented by the concept of divine organization. It means the right people, in the right place, at the right time, and doing the right thing. Putting order into practice means keeping a tidy home and workspace, decluttering our minds by setting clear goals, and being organized in all aspects of our lives. When we have order, we have clarity and peace of mind.

4. Harmony (Reciprocity)

Harmony is the concept of living in peace and balance with others. It means treating others with kindness, respect, and compassion while embracing our interdependence. When we live in harmony, we recognize that our actions affect others and vice versa. We aim to create positive interactions and relationships while avoiding harm to ourselves and others.

5. Propriety

Propriety is the principle of ethics and moral conduct. It's about doing the right thing, in the right way, at the right time, for the right reasons. Propriety means being responsible for our actions, words, and intentions. When we practice propriety, we act with humility and respect, valuing and acknowledging the contributions of others. We also strive to maintain our dignity and self-respect, treating others how we want to be treated and upholding moral and ethical standards.

6. Sincerity

Sincerity is the principle of authenticity in all our interactions. It's about speaking the truth with conviction and acting in line with our values and beliefs. Practicing sincerity means being true to yourself, your beliefs, and your emotions. It also means being kind, compassionate, and respectful to others, acknowledging their feelings and opinions, and communicating openly and honestly.

7. Wisdom

Wisdom is the pinnacle of Maat's principles. It means using knowledge and experience to make informed decisions and act with sound judgment. When we live in wisdom, we learn from our experiences and share our learnings with others. We seek knowledge and understanding and use them to make well-informed decisions and act thoughtfully.

The principles of Maat represent a holistic approach to living a purposeful and fulfilled life. By applying these principles, we can create a just and equitable society where people can live in peace, harmony, and balance. These principles remind us to stay true to our values, acknowledge our interdependence with others, and act with wisdom and integrity. We find inner harmony and live meaningful lives when we embrace these principles.

Spiritual Implications of Maat

The concept of Ma'at has been a central theme in Egyptian society for thousands of years. Ma'at represents the principles of order, balance, and harmony in nature and human affairs. It has guided the actions of Egyptian rulers, priests, and everyday citizens, and it remains a powerful force with spiritual implications that are just as relevant today. Let's explore the spiritual implications of Ma'at and how it can help us lead more fulfilling lives.

Ma'at is not just a concept but a goddess who embodies the principles of Ma'at. She is depicted as a woman with a feather in her hair, symbolizing the importance of balance and truth. When Egyptians lived by the principles of Ma'at, they believed they would be rewarded with a happy afterlife. The spiritual implications of Ma'at, therefore, are closely linked to the idea of karma. How we live our lives will impact our future, whether it be in this life or the next.

Living by the principles of Ma'at means leading a life of balance and harmony. It means being truthful and honest in our dealings with others and striving for justice and equality. It also means being responsible for ourselves and the world around us. This can be seen in the ancient Egyptian concept of ma Heka, which means "true words and strong magic." It suggests that our words and actions have a powerful impact on the world around us.

One of the spiritual implications of Ma'at is the importance of accepting responsibility for our actions. Living by Ma'at means acknowledging that we are responsible for our fate and that our actions have consequences. This concept can be difficult to accept, but it is crucial for personal growth and spiritual development. When we take responsibility for our actions, we are empowered to make positive changes in our lives and the lives of those around us.

Another implication of Ma'at is the importance of nurturing our relationships with others. Ma'at encourages us to treat others with kindness and respect, as we would like to be treated ourselves. It is a reminder to put ourselves in others' shoes and to be empathetic and compassionate. By nurturing our relationships with others, we promote a sense of community and interconnectedness essential for spiritual growth.

Ma'at also encourages us to embrace change and evolution. Egyptian mythology tells the story of the Phoenix, a mythical bird reborn from its ashes. This story symbolizes the transformative power of change and the importance of letting go of what no longer serves us. By embracing change and evolution, we can grow spiritually and emotionally and lead more fulfilling lives.

The spiritual implications of Ma'at are vast and far-reaching. Its principles of balance, truth, and harmony continue to guide us on our journey toward personal growth and spiritual development. By following Ma'at, we are empowered to take responsibility for our actions, nurture our relationships with others, and embrace change and evolution. It is a powerful reminder that our words and actions profoundly impact the world around us and that we can create positive change in our own lives and the lives of others.

Ethical and Moral Considerations of Maat

Maat is one of the best sources of wisdom and knowledge for living a healthy and successful life. The modern world has become increasingly complex and presents ethical and moral dilemmas. Therefore, adopting Maat can provide a moral compass and guidance that is relevant and applicable in the world today. Maat is a comprehensive philosophy that applies to every aspect of human life. It covers all of life, the physical, the spiritual, the social, and the emotional. Its value system is based on the principles of harmony, balance, and order. Maat teaches that one can achieve a fulfilled and purposeful life by honoring these virtues. Moreover, the philosophy offers guidelines to ensure that decisions and actions align with the virtues.

Honesty is one of Maat's essential principles. It is essential to all aspects of life- personal, professional, and spiritual. Being honest promotes trust and reliability and fosters healthy relationships. However, it comes with a price. Honesty requires courage and can lead to personal vulnerability and other risks. Therefore, when considering whether to be truthful, Maat's philosophy proposes balancing the virtue of honesty with compassion and understanding.

Another core principle of Maat's philosophy is justice. Justice is any action that brings balance back into a situation that is out of balance. The role of justice includes preventing harm, mitigating damage, and instilling accountability. Maat's philosophy believes that justice must be applied equally and without bias. Therefore, before making a judgment or taking action, It suggests considering facts, truth, and wisdom to ensure that actions are just.

Respect is also a significant principle in Maat's philosophy. It involves treating all beings in the world with dignity, fairness, and impartiality. This ethic is essential because it shapes how we interact and respond to the diversity of people and situations in our lives. Respect also fosters unity and demonstrates our commitment to upholding the universal values of Maat.

The concept of Maat recognizes the importance of spirituality in life. The principle of spirituality is not based on dogma or doctrine but on personal growth and development. Everyone has a unique path and journey to live to their fullest potential. Therefore, discovering what spirituality means to us individually is essential for our fulfillment, growth, and purpose.

Adopting Maat's philosophy can significantly impact our lives and provide us with a moral compass that is relevant and applicable today. The principles of honesty, justice, respect, balance, and spirituality can guide us in decision-making and our interactions with the world around us. The concrete application of these principles can lead us toward a fulfilling life and create a better world for all beings. So, let us consider adopting the Maat philosophy and making the world a better place!

Chapter 5:

Festivals, Prayers, and Sacrifices

Ancient Egyptians celebrated their beloved concept of Maat through festivals, prayers, and sacrifices. Every year, cities throughout Egypt held grand festivals, which frequently included parades featuring gods in the form of statues carried on boats down the Nile River. Long and reverential prayers were also said to encourage everyone to live with justice and fairness. Valuable items were sacrificed as an offering to the gods in hopes of gaining Maat's blessings. Together, these acts provided a sense of joy and renewal for Egyptians as they expressed their appreciation for harmony and balance.

This chapter will explore the various festivals and ceremonies dedicated to Maat, from ancient Egypt to modern practitioners. It will provide an overview of how to offer prayers and sacrifices to Maat properly. The festivals and rituals associated with Maat demonstrate the importance of this concept to the ancient Egyptians. Exploring these ancient customs makes it possible to understand the great importance of honoring Maat.

Ancient Egyptian Festivals

Ancient Egypt is renowned for its rich cultural heritage that continues to fascinate people across the globe. One of the most impactful aspects of their culture was their festival celebrations. Ancient Egyptians would often commemorate their gods, goddesses, and milestones with vibrant festivals that offered a window into their religious beliefs and way of life. Here are some of the most significant festivals that helped shape Ancient Egypt's cultural identity!

1. The Opet Festival

The Opet Festival, known as one of the oldest religious festivals in Ancient Egypt, was a 27-day-long celebration that took place annually in Thebes. The festival honored the union of Amun and his consort Mut and aimed to reinforce the pharaoh's legitimacy. The main event was the procession of the statues of Amun, Mut, and their son Khonsu carried down the Nile with dancing, singing, and feasting.

2. The Wepet Renpet Festival

The Wepet Renpet Festival, or the "Opening of the Year," was an essential six-day celebration that marked the start of the New Year in Ancient Egypt. The festival began with the prediction of the Nile's flood through offerings of cattle, bread, and water. On the fourth day, people exchanged gifts, and children were gifted with small toys symbolizing rebirth and the new year.

3. The Sed Festival

The Sed Festival, also known as the Heb Sed Festival, was a celebration that honored the pharaoh's thirty-year rule. The festival aimed to strengthen the royal family's authority, renew the pharaoh's divine powers, and confirm their legitimacy to rule. The main event was the "Sed Run," a race the pharaoh would complete to prove his vitality and fitness to continue ruling.

4. 4. The Beautiful Feast of the Valley

The Beautiful Feast of the Valley was a significant annual festival in Thebes. It was a time to pay homage to the deceased relatives and honor the dead, who were believed to travel back to earth during this time. It was a period filled with singing, dancing, and rituals of purification designed to encourage the dead to lead a prosperous life.

5. The Nefertiti Festival

The Nefertiti festival was a religious celebration of exceptional significance. The cult of Nefertiti, the beautiful queen of Akhenaten, was celebrated annually in her honor to ensure her continued favor with the gods. An integral part of the festival was the presentation of offerings, including food and drink, and the performance of sacred music in the temple.

Ancient Egypt was home to some of the world's most prominent festivals dedicated to celebrating their gods, goddesses, and cultural milestones. These vibrant events were an essential part of their religious beliefs and a reflection of their way of life. Whether it was the Opet Festival or the Nefertiti Festival, these celebrations continue to inspire us to celebrate our achievements and express gratitude for our past.

Rituals and Practices Devoted to Maat

Throughout ancient Egyptian history, the goddess Maat was known as the personification of truth, justice, and harmony. As such, people offered her praise and introduced various formal rituals and practices devoted to her. Let's delve deep into the significance and meaning of rituals and practices devoted to Maat. We will also explore the goddess's background and how she became such an influential figure in ancient Egyptian society.

Maat was a goddess not associated with any particular town or city. Instead, her sphere of influence was the entire universe, and her principles of order and virtue permeated every part of Egyptian society. Throughout history, the Egyptians praised her through various rituals and practices, including meditation, divination, and prayer. These practices were dedicated to honoring her and adhering to her principles of order and balance.

One of the most popular rituals devoted to Maat was the weighing of the heart ceremony. In ancient Egyptian belief, after death, the deceased person's heart would be weighed against the feather of Maat. The ceremony was meant to determine if the person had lived a life in Maat's principles of truth, justice, and harmony. If the person passed the test, they would be granted eternal life in the afterlife.

This ritual was so crucial to the ancient Egyptians that it was included in the Egyptian Book of the Dead.

Another significant practice devoted to Maat is the offering of food and libations. In ancient Egypt, people believed that the gods nourished themselves on the offerings made to them. As such, people offered Maat fruits, vegetables, bread, beer, and wine, amongst other things. The people believed that the practice of offering these items would bring balance, harmony, and prosperity to their lives.

Moreover, meditation and divination were also vital practices devoted to Maat. People believed that meditation on Maat's principles and using divination tools such as Tarot cards and oracle bones would help them gain deeper insights into their lives. This knowledge would enable them to live their lives guided by Maat's principles.

Crafting Prayers and Offerings

Maat's name means "that which is straight," reflecting her role in upholding justice and maintaining order in the world. One way to honor Maat is to craft prayers and offerings that reflect her qualities and attributes. The significance of prayers and offerings in the Kemetic religion cannot be overstated. Prayers to the gods were an essential aspect of Egyptian religion, and offerings were made to provide sustenance for the gods. Offerings were seen as a way to establish a relationship between the gods and the people. To honor Maat, practitioners may create an altar dedicated to her and offer a variety of items such as candles, incense, or jewelry. Offerings of food, water, or flowers are also common.

Crafting effective prayers and offerings for Maat involves reflecting on her qualities and attributes. For instance, those offering to Maat may consider the role of justice in their own lives or community. They may reflect on the importance of balance in their practice and offer items reflecting this, like a scale. Similarly, prayers may focus on asking for guidance or support in maintaining justice and balance in their lives. Practitioners may also craft prayers that reflect gratitude for the work of Maat in the world and her presence in their own daily lives.

In addition to crafting effective prayers and offerings, practitioners may wish to consider the ritual or ceremonial aspect of their practice. Creating a sacred space through the use of candles, music, or incense can increase the power of a prayer or offering. It is also crucial to consider the timing of the prayer or offering in alignment with the seasons, lunar phases, or significant dates in ancient Egyptian history.

By reflecting on her qualities and attributes, practitioners can deepen their practice and relationship with Maat. Taking time to create a sacred space and consider the ritual or ceremonial aspect of offerings can also enhance the power and significance of the practice. As modern followers of ancient Egyptian religion, we are privileged to continue to honor and offer to deities like Maat, carrying forward the traditions and beliefs of our ancestors.

Traditional Sacrifices

To maintain Maat's goodwill, people offered her traditional sacrifices. These rituals and practices ensured that everything in their lives remained in harmony and under her protection. Here are some of the sacrifices they used to offer:

Incense

One of the most common traditional sacrifices for Maat was the offering of incense. People would burn sweet-smelling substances like myrrh, frankincense, and various flowers to create fragrant smoke, which they believed could reach the goddess's realm and please her. These offerings were usually made at temples dedicated to Maat but also in people's homes, especially during special occasions like feasts or important life events.

Food and Earthly Goods

Another traditional sacrifice for Maat was offering food and other earthly goods. People believed that the goddess enjoyed the same things humans did, so they would offer a wide range of food, beverages, and other commodities in her name. Some of the most popular offerings included bread, wine, water, beer, fruits, vegetables, and meat. These offerings were usually left in front of her statues or altars. Sometimes they would be buried in the ground as a symbol of returning them to the earth where they came from.

Donations

People also used to perform various acts of service or vows to honor Maat. These could involve donating money or materials to the temple, carrying out charitable deeds like feeding the poor or clothing the needy, or undertaking special tasks or challenges in her name. These offerings were believed to demonstrate one's devotion and loyalty to the goddess and were often accompanied by prayers, dances, or other sacred rituals.

Living Virtuously

In addition to these traditional sacrifices, people also believed they could appease Maat by avoiding negative actions and thoughts that disrupted the natural order of things. This included acts like lying, stealing, cheating, or causing harm to others and cultivating virtues like truthfulness, generosity, kindness, and respect for others. By living a life in harmony with Maat's ideals and values, people hoped to ensure her protection and blessings.

The traditional sacrifices for Maat were an essential part of ancient Egyptian religious practices, as they helped people maintain harmony and balance. Although these rituals may seem outdated or superstitious to modern observers, they are a testament to the enduring human desire for connection with something greater than oneself. By reflecting on these practices and the values they embody, we can better understand our shared human experiences and the importance of maintaining balance and order in our lives.

Appropriate Prayers for Maat

Offering prayers and honoring this ancient Egyptian goddess is a way of connecting with the divine and seeking balance and order in our lives. But as with any spiritual practice, it's crucial to approach it with respect and mindfulness. Let's explore the different types of prayers you can offer to Maat, how to do it with a proper tone of voice, and some tips on creating a sacred space for your prayers.

1. What Prayers to Offer

Maat was the goddess of balance, truth, and justice, so any prayer that aligns with those values would be appropriate. You can ask Maat to help you achieve balance in your life, to grant you the courage to speak the truth, or to guide you towards a just resolution of a situation. You can also offer gratitude and praise for how Maat has brought harmony and order to your life.

2. How To Offer Prayers

When offering prayers to Maat, it's vital to come from a place of sincerity and respect. You can light candles, burn incense, or use other symbols that resonate with you to create a sacred space. Sit or stand comfortably with good posture, and focus your mind and attention on Maat. Offer your prayers in a tone of voice that is gentle, respectful, and clear. Remember to breathe deeply and allow space for listening and receiving any guidance or wisdom.

3. Tone of Voice

Your tone of voice is an integral aspect of offering prayers to Maat. A respectful and reverent tone helps create a sacred atmosphere and signals your intention to honor Maat. Avoid using a loud or hurried tone, as this may come across as insincere or disrespectful. Instead, use a tone that is calm, clear, and deliberate. It's also crucial to vary your tone with the content of your prayer. Expressing gratitude and praise may require a higher, lighter tone, while asking for guidance or help may require a deeper and more solemn tone.

4. Creating a Sacred Space

Creating a sacred space can help you focus your energy and attention when offering prayers to Maat. Symbols, such as candles, incense, or crystals, create a visual centerpiece. Choose a space that is quiet, clean, and free from distractions. You can also decorate your space with images or statues of Maat or other symbols that resonate with you. Remember to clear any negative or stagnant energy from your space before your prayer session.

Offering prayers to Maat is a powerful way of seeking balance, truth, and justice in our lives. We can connect with the divine and invite Maat's guidance and wisdom by approaching this practice with sincerity, respect, and mindfulness. Remember to offer prayers that align with Maat's values, use a respectful and clear tone of voice, and create a sacred space that is conducive to your practice. With these simple steps, you can begin to honor Maat and invite her into your daily life.

Maat's principles of truth, justice, and harmony have remained significant to the ancient Egyptians and modern-day religious devotees. People worldwide have carried forward various rituals and practices devoted to this goddess, reflecting her philosophical and spiritual importance in their cultures. Whether you believe in Maat or not, it's clear that the rituals and practices devoted to her have a lot to offer in terms of establishing a balance in life. So, let us all incorporate some of these practices of Maat into our daily lives and embrace the teachings of truth, justice, and harmony to live more fulfilling lives.

Conclusion

Maat was a core part of life in ancient Egypt and continues to be essential to the modern understanding of the period. This ethical system of law set the bar for behavior, bringing clarity to everyday living through its focus on truths, justice, and social customs. Pharaohs followed this same code while being expected to uphold high standards and protect their citizens. They supported all communities with Maat's tenants firmly in mind. By doing so, a seamless connection between gods, humans, and rulers allowed such an incredible civilization to thrive. To this day, Egyptologists continue examining the role of Maat in ancient Egypt's impressive history and how it informs current practices.

The ancient Egyptians believed that the god Atum created Maat, and many other gods and goddesses were closely linked to it. These divine entities included Ra, Horus, Isis, Thoth, and Anubis, who represent the various principles of Maat. All these gods have been associated with upholding honest and just practices. They provided a great spiritual influence on both pilgrims and everyday people. The temples honoring these gods have become timeless destinations for those looking to understand more about Egyptian culture. Their stories remain inspiring today as reminders of what qualities societies should strive towards to live harmoniously.

Festivals, prayers, and sacrifices in honor of Maat have been practiced for centuries. It is an integral part of ancient Egyptian religious life and upholds its core principles of balance and justice. Those who celebrated Maat would take part in several ritual activities, including offerings to the gods associated with it, such as Thoth and Amun-Ra, as well as performing music and dance. Such festivals served to remind worshippers that even though chaos may reign from time to time, the universe was ultimately held in balance by Maat's laws, and it's essential to uphold them in our everyday lives. Celebrating Maat reminds people of this timeless truth.

Maat remained an important part of Egyptian culture and religion even after the collapse of their civilization. In modern times, many people have studied Maat and its teachings to understand the ancient Egyptians better. It remains a source of inspiration for many people today, who strive to live according to its principles of truth, justice, and balance. It serves as a reminder that no matter how much time passes, Maat's influence and teachings will continue to shape our lives.

This guide to Maat will discuss its history, its principles, and the gods associated with it. You have now learned how Maat was celebrated in ancient Egypt and how you can use its teachings to enrich your life today. We hope you find it enlightening!

References

Aladdin, A. (n.d.). Ma'at Egyptian god - ma'at, the god of justice. Ask Aladdin, The Middle East Travel Experts Guides. https://www.ask-aladdin.com/all-destinations/egypt/category/ancient-egyptian-gods/page/maat-the-god-of-justice

Goddess Maat. (2022, January 16). Landious Travel. https://landioustravel.com/egypt/egyptian-deities/goddess-maat/

Hill, B. (2019, June 9). Maat: Ancient Egyptian goddess of truth, justice, and morality. Ancient Origins. https://www.ancient-origins.net/history-ancient-traditions/maat-ancient-egyptian-goddess-truth-justice-and-morality-003131

Ma'at. (n.d.). Egyptianmuseum.org. https://egyptianmuseum.org/deities-Maat

Mark, J. J. (2016). Ma'at. World History Encyclopedia. https://www.worldhistory.org/Ma' at/

No title. (n.d.). Study.com. https://study.com/academy/lesson/maat-definition-principles-in-ancient-egypt.html

The Editors of Encyclopedia Britannica. (2023). Maat. In Encyclopedia Britannica.

Wigington, P. (2009, August 6). Ma'at, Egyptian goddess of truth and balance. Learn Religions. https://www.learnreligions.com/the-egyptian-goddess-maat-2561790

9 798215 753743